How To Make Your Money Last

20 Tips to Get you to Retirement faster!

Introduction

I want to thank you and congratulate you for downloading the book, *"How to Make Your Money Last: 20 Tips to Get You to Retirement Faster!"*

This book contains proven steps and strategies on how to financially prepare you for retirement!

The elderly years are one of the most challenging phases of life...it can be an age when all the fatigue of the life seems to have struck you all at once.

This is the age when your financial situation is tested the most. Your body may not allow you to work as hard as you used to while you were young, but your financial needs will only see an upward curve considering the increase in medical bills and lifestyle costs that you might have to pay at that age.

It is because of these reasons that people worry about not having enough money saved to enjoy their golden years. However, this will not be the case for you if you start planning and saving early.

The first step towards making your money last is to squeeze money out of your assets.

If you have a good amount of savings, take out a little money from it every year and invest it to get periodic returns. Besides this, pension accounts, home equity and retirement account are also your assets that you can manipulate. Planning it right will surely help you grow your money with time and allow it to survive longer with you.

One of the thinking patterns that I notice in people is that they believe they aren't young enough to start saving and the time for them to implement any saving plans is gone. It is vital for you to understand that no matter where you stand in your financial journey, you can almost always make a turn around. Remember that big changes start with small steps. With this said, nobody would disagree to the fact that the first step is usually the hardest step to take.

In order to help you make the first step and many more steps towards a secured post-retirement life, we have here a list of 20 tips that you can use and implement in your day-to-day life. Although, none of these tips is a masterstroke that will change your financial condition completely, each one of them will bring you closer to your goal in a big way.

So, how much of time and effort will these require on your part? While some of the tips may just require a few minutes of your time, others may demand regular effort. With this said, none of the tips will be too tough for you incorporate in your life or schedule. They are fairly simple!

Another important thing that is worth mentioning here is that some of the tips given here may not even apply to you. This doesn't mean that the book is not for you. From the list of 20, you will surely find a subset of 10-15 tips that apply to you. You can get started with these tips and see the changes that they can bring to your life. Certainly, you will end up saving much more money that you could have ever thought.

Tip #1: Perform Better Bank Management For Better Financial Management

Banks can lure you in with offers like no monthly fees for using a debit card and increased interest rates. Keeping yourself updated with the newest offers in the financial market can help you earn higher interest. Moreover, you may also save some money on the way.

Whenever possible, make an online bill payment from the bank directly. This will help you in two ways. Firstly, it will save you the running around and travelling to the respective offices to drop off a check. Secondly, you will not be required to pay the draft fee, an extra amount over and above the payment value. In addition, an added benefit to you is that you will not have to buy stamps and other added requirements for making a payment.

If you are a credit card user, you may end up paying a good amount of money in interest to the bank. As a customer, you must know that you also have some power in your hands. The credit card issuers are usually open to negotiations as far as interest rates are concerned. In addition, they also have balance transfer schemes to transfer the balance of your card to a different card.

You can simply call your credit card company and enquire if they offer any of these facilities. Understand that you are the customer and it is your right to determine the terms of the contract. If you don't agree with certain terms, you have the right to communicate the issues and the credit card company is obligated to respond to you.

Tip #2: Saving Starts At Home!

Home is where you spend most of your time, be it sleeping, relaxing or spending time with friends and family. While all of us love a comfortable life and don't wish to compromise on it in any way, some small steps can help you save volumes in your bill.

To start with, the biggest and heaviest bill that we pay includes water and electricity bills. You can cut down on the electricity units consumed in your house by ensuring that you turn off the television if no one is watching, turning of the lights if no one is at home and saving water, which is not just a monetary saving for you, but a saving of a natural resource as well. The bottom line is that if you are not using something just don't pay for it.

The second kind of expenditure that we make at a regular basis in our homes is grocery. When you don't go prepared with a list, chances are high that you will buy things that you don't need and the actual grocery items will feature nowhere in your bill. What this means is that you will end up spending much more than you should have because grocery is your fundamental expenditure and anything you buy over and above that is most likely wasteful expenditure.

The ground rule here is to prepare a list of the things you need and buy only the things that feature on that list. The list restricts you from buying anything unplanned and potentially unwanted. So, remember to make a list next time you go shopping for grocery and most importantly, stick to the list!

We all are so busy in our lives that people no longer have the time to tuck their buttons or sew a torn shirt. So, what people usually do is that they throw the shirt away, which is not just a wasted resource, but also an extra expenditure. Try and take out the time to sew that torn shirt or tuck the broken button to use your clothes.

Sewing is not a big job and even if you have no idea of how it is done, picking it up from a simple online tutorial should not be tough. Learning a few of these skills and adopting them for your day-to-day issues can be a great way to save money and make your stuff last much longer.

In line with this suggestion, you can also try to fix little issues like a blocked pipe or a malfunctioned light bulb yourself. All of these jobs are also simple things that you will pick up easily. Consequently, you won't be dependent on the electrician or plumber for little tasks and save money as well.

Tip #3: Shop Smartly

You will have to buy stuff for your house, be it for grocery or items for personal use. The ground rule is shop for stuff that you need and not just anything you like over the counter. Understandably, the cravings and temptation can be difficult to overcome. In order to help you address this issue, we have a 30-day plan for you.

Whenever you plan to buy anything, be sure to wait for a minimum time of 30 days to decide on the purchase. There is a high probability that you will decide on not buying the article after this time if you don't really need it. This strategy will help you buy only the stuff that you require and not just because you have an urge to buy it. Moreover, if you still plan on buying the item, you would have had the right perspective of the purchase.

Once you have decided that you need to buy an item, it is time to look for deals that are offering best value for money. Yard sales are some great places to find good deals. However, be extremely careful while shopping at sales as lowered prices tempt people to buy a lot of the stuff that you had not planned to buy perhaps don't even know. So, even if it is a sale, only buy the items that are there on your list.

If you don't have a sale running in your locality, another option to cut down on the total cost is to compare the prices that different stores are offering. Most stores compete with each other to give the lowest cost. This is their own way to attract customers. However, you can take advantage of this by comparing the prices and buying stuff from the store that is offering the lowest cost.

It might be difficult to track the cost of each and every item on the grocery list. Therefore, you may pick out 20 or so items that you buy on a regular basis and keep track of the prices offered by different stores for that item. In this manner, you will get maximum benefit without putting in a lot of effort.

Stores offer rewards for shopping with them and this can also be a great way to save on the total money spent on buying grocery. The card points can be converted into cash backs or discounts on products that you buy from the respective store.

Beware, however, to not give them the email id that you use for professional purposes or you will end up spamming up your inbox folder on a daily basis. What you can do is that you can create a special email address for emailing lists. As and when you receive coupons on the email address, you can use them and for the rest of the emails, you can just ignore them!

Another piece of advice that we have for you is that sometimes it is better to buy a used item than a bran new one for the simple reason that you wouldn't want to waste your money on buying an new item when the used item will also do the job just as well for you. Well, you can't buy used clothes, but when it comes to furniture for the garage or tools, trying the used option might also be a good idea.

Tip #4: Don't Waste Money On Convenience Foods and Addictions

People have a tendency to get used to eating convenience food like fast food for the sheer ease that is associated with them. However, with all the ease all comes a lot of disadvantages. Items like prepackaged dinner are not just unhealthy for you, but it is also costly. A simple meal made at home is much healthier and low-cost.

On similar lines, you must replace all the cold drinks and beverages you drink with water. Drinking a good amount of water has a plenty of health benefits. For instance, water detoxifies the body and feeds the body organs with its required hydration. Apart from moving towards a healthier body, a bottle of water will cost you lesser than soda, juice or tea. Contrary to popular belief, tap water is also clean and comes for no cost.

The last thing that falls under this category is smoking and alcohol consumption. Both these habits affect you gravely so much so that they may lead you to chronic diseases and even death. In addition to the grave consequences that these habits may make you face, they are expensive habits to maintain.

If you have been a chain smoker or regular drinker, try to reduce your consumption and see how it impacts your health and financial condition. You may have to face real difficulty getting rid of these habits, but a strong will power and motivation for the good should help you sail through. Besides this, you also have rehabilitation camps to help you overcome these addictions if you feel the need for external help.

Tip #5: Buy Only What You Need

You don't have to buy everything you need, particularly the things that you need on a temporary basis. For instance, you can get books, CDs and DVDs on rent and swap them with other ones after you are done reading or watching these. You can also enroll yourself to a local library to get the required resources. This will obviously help you save money if you compare the situation with buying each and every book and DVD or CD you want.

Other than books and CDs/DVDs, people also spend a lot of money in buying video games. If you also fall under this category of people, we recommend that you focus on buying video games that you can play for a longer time. Moreover, make it a point to master a game before you think about buying a new video game.

Some games that have a longer shelf life than others are puzzles and quest games. After you have mastered the game and no longer feel the need to play the game anymore, you can choose to resell the game at the local Game Shop and buy a new game using this money.

We all need gifts to give on birthdays and special occasions to friends and family. Instead of buying an expensive gift, think about making a personalized gift for your loved ones. While this will convey your thoughts appropriately to the person, who is exactly what gifts are all about, it will also help you save a lot of money.

Some beautiful gifts that you can create at home include candles, food mixes, soaps and cookies or cakes. All these things can be made at home without the need for you to spend a lot of money on them. The personal touch that these gifts give to your thoughts cannot be bought from the best of stores and for even a million dollars. These gifts will be kept, preserved and stored for years to come. Contrary to this, your store-bought gifts will end up in junk or a corner of the closet.

Just like the gifts, there are a lot of things that you use and you can make at home. Like we said, most of bakery items like cakes, cookies and candles or soaps can be easily made at home. Moreover, homemade products are much better than their commercial counterparts and they cost much less, saving you a lot of money.

Tip #6: Sell Off The Extras

The times when collectibles were in fashion and people believed that their collections would bring them a huge fortune in time. However, with the change in age and time, collectibles have lost their value so much so that most of these collectibles can easily be found online for a price way lower than what their initial cost was. So, people who had spent thousands of dollars in buying those collectibles would have regretted.

In other words, if you have items that have questionable value, then it better to sell them off. It will get you some money and help you get rid of extra clutter in your house. Besides this, you will also be able to get back a fraction of the money that you would have spent on buying the item.

When we talk about clutter, the one place that is the heart of all clutter in the world is the closet. It is a good idea to screen your closet at a regular basis and mark out the things that you no longer use. You don't have to throw it away. You can donate it to the needy and claim a tax deduction. You may avail of these options to make and save money from the stuff that you already own.

Tip #7: Save Energy, Save Money!

One of our essential expenditures is electricity, water and utility bills. You can reduce these bills by making some proactive efforts. The first thing is to replace the bulbs used in the house with energy-efficient bulbs. Although, these bulbs will cost you more than the other bulbs, they will help you save volumes in the long run by helping you save electricity.

There are many types of these light bulbs available in the market. It might not be easy for you to decide which bulb to buy. However, irrespective of the type you buy, rest assured that you would have an upgrade and a lowered electricity bill than usual.

To give you an overview of the options available to you, there are two main categories of energy-efficient bulbs namely, CFLs and LEDs. CFLs cost a little more than conventional bulbs and lower than LEDs. Moreover, the energy consumed by these bulbs is 25% of the energy consumed by conventional bulbs.

However, these bulbs suffer from an inherent drawback. These bulbs contain some mercury and it takes some time to glow up to the brightness promised. Glowing of the bulb is a gradual process and you will have to live with it to save 75% of electricity units.

In the event that you don't wish to compromise on the drawbacks of CFLs, you can go for LEDs, which are a little more expensive than CFLs. These are undoubtedly the best lighting option available in the market. Research is underway to lower the cost of these bulbs and the day is not far when these bulbs will cost much lower. These bulbs are just as efficient as the LEDs and do not require any time to glow up to maximum light. If the idea of changing all the bulbs in the house all at once is baffling you, you may change a few bulbs every month until all the bulbs are changed. This will keep you tucked up to your budget and plan better for the future.

One of the biggest advantages of using energy-efficient bulbs is that they last for years because of their quality. Just like these bulbs, you must take care of the fact that you check the quality of any appliance that you buy. It is better to pay a little more for good-quality appliances that last longer than appliances that you will need to replace every now and then.

Every single time you plan to buy an appliance, be sure to check if the appliance is energy-efficient. Besides this, always do some research on the available options and see how the options outdo each other before zeroing down on one option. The same principle applies to cars and conveyance.

Tip #8: Maintain Your Machinery To Make It Last Longer And Work Better

Buying a good quality machine and leaving it to the mercy of nature will reduce its life. You cannot blame nature for not maintaining your equipment. Therefore, if you don't maintain your stuff, no matter how expensive and good-quality stuff you buy, you will have to replace it. For example, you must clean the filters of your car and air conditioners at a regular basis. If need be, you may change these filters before they completely damage your device.

It is a good idea to perform a maintenance run for all your devices and appliances. Get rid of the dust clogging to them and ensure that they are cleaned regularly. Appliances like dryers, coolers and air conditioners have vents. Blockage of these vents can cause serious damage to your device. Therefore, give the required attention to these aspects of appliance cleaning. The better these appliances function, the lesser energy they will consume and the lower you will have to pay for your electricity bills and maintenance/replacement costs.

Tip #9 Avoid Stress-Spending

With women, it is a common tendency to go shopping every time they feel stressed or bored. In fact, some people consider spending money anti-depressive. All of these are just fallacies and such a thought will rarely be a good idea. You must look for better and more cost-effective ways to de-stress yourself. For instance, breathing exercises and yoga/meditation can be of great help.

Another important thing that you must guard against is casual visits to the mall. The mall is a great way to hang around, meet friends and watch people. However, the mall is also a place of temptation. You shouldn't visit the mall unless you have a list of things to buy. Window-shopping is a great time pass, but this can be torturous activity for people on a budget. Instead of making those random visits to the mall, you can go on an adventure, take a walk in the park or pick up a hobby. These options will be much more constructive.

Tip #10 Cancel Unused Memberships

Do you know the membership business model is such a successful proposition? It is for the simple that a membership once bought is never lost; it is only renewed. The anticipation that you might need it next year keeps you from cancelling it. However, if you are not using a membership, go ahead and cancel. When you didn't use it all this while, you wouldn't need it in the future too. With this said, if you do require it in the future, you have an option to renew the membership whenever you want.

The same principle applies to magazine memberships. All of us have memberships and enrollments that we have made and forgotten. The membership amount is usually so low that we don't even bother cancelling them. However, each spending counts. Therefore, get rid of any expenditure that is not required and this will surely be high up in your list.

Tip #11: Insurance Is Not Savings!

Most of us buy insurance as a substitute of savings or investment. However, the truth is that when you give money for getting insured, you are just dumping money that might come to use if a mishap occurs. With that said, there is no way you can get the money back in the event that nothing happens.

So, when choosing a term life insurance, be sure to compare the different plans and choose a plan that is value for money. Whole-life policies cost more and return nothing on lapsing. Therefore, it is wiser to choose insurance plan that costs less and solves the purpose for you.

Tip #12: Avoid Online Shopping

The one technology that has revolutionized the way we shop and buy stuff is online shopping. Buying stuff was never simpler. However, if you view the situation from another perspective, spending money was never simpler than this. You have your credit card information saved in your accounts and you just need an instinctive click to buy anything. Whether you needed these items or not are thoughts that will appear much after your payment has been made.

Therefore, never keep your credit card information saved in your online shopping accounts. Filling in information every single time allows you the time to think if the purchase is really required. The one extra step that you have to perform when the card information is not there might just be the time when you realize that the item is not required.

In order to make worthy purchases, you can also follow what is called the '10-seconds rule'. Whenever you decide to make a buy and add an item to the cart, give yourself a 10 seconds time before checkout to ask yourself if you really need this product. If you can't answer this question or get a no, you can cancel the order right away. This is a great way to avoid impulse buys.

Tip #13: Rent Out Your Space

Do you have an empty garage or an empty floor or apartment? If yes, then you can also think about renting out this space. This will certainly bring you big money. With websites that directly connect real estate owners to potential renters or visitors, renting spaces has become extremely simple. You can make a search online to check the sites that offer such functionality.

Tip #14: Keep A Tab On Your Debt

When it comes to finances and financial planning, the one thing that you need to fear the most is 'debt'. This becomes an even bigger problem when you have debt on you that you have to repay and no extra money in your hand to do it. Therefore, it is always a good idea to keep a tab on the debt that is on you at any time. Make regular debt calculations to keep the pressure going on you to save.

Tip #15: Manage Your Meals

If there is one thing after accommodation and utility bills that eat up a chunk of your money, it is food! This is all the more true for people who regularly eat out. Making food at home is much cheaper and healthier than the best of food joints can offer you.

Therefore, before you leave home, make it a point to eat breakfast. This will keep your stomach filled and help you avoid the mid-meal snacks. In addition, pack yourself lunch and take it to school or work. This will help you save from a lot of your daily expenditure. Notwithstanding, this lunch will be healthier and packed with all the goodness in the world.

When you make your lunch in the morning, you can try a quick recipe and also include leftovers from the last night's dinner to reduce the waste and give your lunch a hint of uniqueness. Foods like leftover turkey used in a sandwich makes excellent recipes. You cannot perhaps realize this until you try it.

It is customary to take your friends out for lunches or treats on your birthday or a special occasion. You usually end up with huge bills after the party to pay. It is only when you realize that a party thoughtfully organized at home can be much more fun and cost effective, that you will really be able to share your happiness with your family and friends.

Tip #16: Use Public Transportation

Buying a car is not as expensive an endeavor as maintaining it. The price of the fuel is towering high and you end up paying just as much money on your fuel expense as the cost of the car in a few years. This can be a tragic arrangement if you travel to work alone.

If you are also caught in such a situation, you can try local public transport. It will help you save fuel and cut your transport costs dramatically. Even if you can't make a complete switch to public transport, you may start with a few days in a week kind of arrangement.

Some people don't like the idea of travelling in public transport. Moreover, the public transport systems of some countries are not up to the mark and there may not even a route that connects your office to your home directly. If this is the case, you may team up with a few of your colleagues and carpool with them. The per-head transport cost will reduce to 1/5th its value, which is certainly a substantial saving.

Tip #17: Do Stuff Yourself

Gone are the days when people had the time to maintain gardens, water plants and keep a tab on the growth of their plantations on a daily basis. Although, you may not be able to do all these, what you can still pursue is a small kitchen garden.

While gardening is a great way to de-stress and pass your time, it will also give you free vegetables and herbs for your kitchen. So, you will not have to buy herbs for seasoning and tomatoes for pastes anymore. This will not only save money for you, but it will also give you a taste of freshness and originality like no other.

Tip #18: Stop Using Plastic Money

One of the pioneering reasons why we spend so much is because spending money has become extremely simple. You don't have to go to the bank to withdraw money anymore. All you need is your credit card, which can be swiped for any transaction anywhere. While keeping a credit card for emergencies is a great idea, using credit card everywhere can spell trouble for your finances. You are endlessly increasing the debt on you with every purchase. Therefore, no matter how tempted you may be to use your credit card, avoid using it for random purchases.

Tip #19: Don't Let Mistakes Stop You

It is not easy to get used to a new way of spending money or curbing temptations when you have a latest collection of your favorite brand rolled out. However, when you are on a budget; you are on a budget! There will be times when you will trip off and make a random buy.

This mistake should not keep you from following the 'on a budget' protocol'. Moreover, you should not go about making mistakes and forgive yourself to make another mistakes. Remember your mistakes and make a conscious effort to not repeat them again.

Tip #20: Never Ever Give Up

Debts can be difficult to deal with and unless you make an effort to bring the debt amount down, it will always point upwards. Every time you feel that you cannot keep up with your debt issues, read a blog about managing finances or talk to someone who can inspire you with a personal story. No matter what, keep the fight against debt and the motivation to save, on!

Taking It Forward

Now that you have read through the 20 tips, the next step is to pick out a list of tips that apply to you and that you can incorporate with ease in your lifestyle. It may not be easy and comfortable initially. However, with regular effort, all these tips will become a part of your life. Thinking about your future life and post-retirement convenience, this is just a little sacrifice that you have to make, for a happier and luxurious life ahead.